Architect

of Dreams

A Bridge to the Life You Love

Greg Drolet

GREG DROLET'S ARCHITECT OF DREAMS.

website: gregdrolet.com
email: greg@gregdrolet.com

Cover & Book Design by Morgan Drolet - visit: morgandrolet.com
Cover Photograph by Greg Drolet
Author's Photo by Taylor Herron Photography

ISBN 9-780692-815151

First Edition: December 2016

No artist, whether they are a composer, musician, painter or photographer, can create without a source of passion and inspiration. In my life, I have been blessed with the greatest source of inspiration a man could have, my wife and best friend, Christie, and my son and fellow artist, Morgan.

Daily, they have provided me with a life that others will only dream of. It is through their love, understanding and undying devotion and support that I am able to create the words that they help inspire.

To my Mother and Father, Muriel and Ed, who always told me I could. For your sacrifice, love and teaching I will be eternally thankful.

A special thanks to my wonderful brothers and sisters who taught me so
many valuable lessons.

Introduction

"If nothing changes, nothing changes," yet often times it seems that "the more things change, the more they stay the same."

We all live lives that change by the minute in one way or another. Some of those changes are conscious decisions on our part; other changes are the result of actions taken by others. We can control the former yet cannot ignore the latter, even though we have no control. The direction our lives take will be a result of our attitudes and the decisions we make.

I choose to look at life from a positive perspective, with a belief in my fellow man and the human potential for greatness. Hoping and believing that "out of chaos, comes opportunity." We have the opportunity to rediscover some of the values and virtues of freedom that have been inadvertently buried. I believe that we have the wonderful task of leading the world to a new beginning. A new beginning that causes more people to realize their own mortality, and that none of us can truly live until we come to grips with this inevitable event.

I choose to promote a new world, built daily on understanding and a willingness to serve our fellow man.

I have been fortunate in my life to realize that I needed to surround myself with people who are dreamers and believers, those people with a vision, and the willingness to risk it all to make a difference. Individuals who choose adventure over mediocrity.

God designed us to be great! We are "sons and daughters of a King," and each of us should be compelled to create something we will be proud of in this life and decided to make a difference every day of our lives. It is my hope, that one word, idea or phrase, which I have written will inspire someone to take an action that will make a positive difference in the life of another.

Life is Like a String Instrument

The Master Craftsman meticulously sought out a unique wood that would create a beautifully designed body or instrument. He took time to explore the subtle grain changes that when cut, sanded and lacquered would produce a stunning visual masterpiece that through looks alone would attract people to it's unique characteristics. Then the Master Craftsman, the Artisan of sight and sound, put on strings of various thickness and tuning pegs that would stretch the strings beyond a relaxed, comfortable state and it is in the stretching that each string achieves it's unique and quintessential sound that is similar but different from the other strings on the beautifully designed musical apparatus.

It is this synergistic relationship between various materials and knowledge provided by the Master Craftsman that when properly tuned and put in the hands of the Master Musician that the instrument comes alive with an energy and sound so beautiful that tears of joy will follow.

And yet, left alone and not cared for or caressed, the beautiful instrument will begin to lose its unique qualities. And soon the strings will rust and become slack and the gorgeous wood will lose its luster.

However, hopefully, another Master will come along, see the beauty hidden in a lackluster instrument and begin a process of renovation that will bring back to life the fantastic look and sound originally intended by the Master Craftsman.

Sitting by itself in the corner of a room the unique instrument has all the potential to create tears of joy. But it must be picked up and played by one who can make it come to life. Someone who is willing to put on new strings and retune each unique string that plays a unique note and is a unique part in the creation of a beautiful song.

So it is with each of us. We are unique beings who have been created by the Master Designer, God. We have each been given unique talents that must be continuously explored and tuned. Stretched beyond our comfort zones in order to find the sweet notes we were each intended to produce.

You are a beautiful instrument. Treasure your gifts, explore the possibilities THE Architect of Dreams has instilled in you and create a symphony of life that will make people shed tears of joy for having known you.

Questions to Ponder:

- Why do we avoid stretching?
- Why do we see the beauty and yet not pick up the instrument and explore its possibilities?
- Why do we begin the adventure but then put the instrument in a dark corner or case to collect dust, rust, become slack or fade in color?
- Do we let other's criticism of our playing of the instrument stop/ prevent us from exploring its possibilities?
- Do you believe the instrument was not meant for you? Perhaps another one is, seek it out!
- What music/dreams have you quit chasing and why?

Little Trip

A lesson in writing,
Nary one have I had.
Many who may read this,
Might consider it bad.

But to those who might criticize,
I couldn't give a rip.
I'm designing my world,
I'm on my own little trip!

When You Own the Ship

I sat very quietly, reading the book
That challenged me with a question I could not overlook.
A question so simple and with wisdom did beam
The statement just asked, "Do you own your dream?"

What is your dream? Do you have one my friend?
Can you explain it in detail from beginning to end?
What is your strategy? What action will you take?
Is it a daydreamers dream or a cake that's half-baked?

When you own the ship as Captain you steer,
Headlong into the wind, through storms and through fear.
Believe in yourself! Say YES to your dream.
Tell the world you're a dreamer, your song you must sing.

Love what you do and do what you love.
You've been given a gift from God up above.
You are a miracle, there's only one you.
So what is the dream that you must pursue?

As you travel through time and you come to the end
God will ask you a question you must answer my friend.
Not about toys you collected or were your clothes always in fashion,
But did you own your dream and live it with passion?

"You must be the change you wish to see in the world"
                                                        -Mahatma Ghandi

~ ~ ~ ~

Write down any thoughts you may have regarding the poem or the quote.

_____

_____

_____

_____

_____

_____

_____

_____

_____

What is the dream you have for you life? Take a few minutes to write your
dreams.

_____

_____

_____

_____

_____

_____

_____

_____

_____

The World is Changing

An attack has been made on the U.S. of A,
A tragic event requiring each man to pray.
Pray for the victims, the lives that were lost,
The families and country that paid a great cost.

A terrorist attack on a country so great,
Causing turmoil and chaos unseen to this date.
The cowards who perpetrated this dastardly event,
Have awakened a giant with the message they have sent.

The birthplace of freedom, has come under attack,
A setback for sure, but we are coming back.
The U.S. of A will reply with a force,
Setting our nation on a redefined course.

The question I ask of me and of you,
Is how will you change and what will you do?
About the terrorist inside, which you battle each day,
Will you stay apathetic or enter the fray?

Are you willing to stand up, shake your giant awake?
Cast off the doubt, create a new fate?
We're under attack, it's time to be strong,
Fight for our freedom, righting the wrong!

Our forefathers fought for the freedom we possess,
So stand on their shoulders, call out and confess!
That apathy and laziness are a thing of the past,
We're committed to freedom, a new die has been cast.

Our world has been changed due to this tragic event,
Each of us left to ponder, how our lives will be spent.
Death and destruction, with families no longer intact,
Causing each man to realize, that in life, there is no contract.

What have we done that is exceptional? We should ask.
Then meditate on the answer and define a new task.
What will we do to help change and create,
A world based on love, not destruction and hate?

How do we affect the world that we know?
Hope and compassion should be the seeds that we sow.
What lessons do we teach to the children so young?
It's men and it's women, of integrity, that we want them to become.

Yes, the world it is changing, and we all have a choice,
Stay apathetic or let it hear a strong voice.
A new voice that decided that what needs to be shared,
Is love hope and values, by people who care!

"Every generation needs a new revolution."
-Thomas Jefferson

~ ~ ~ ~

Write down any thoughts you may have regarding the poem or the quote.

_____

_____

_____

_____

_____

_____

_____

_____

_____

_____

What have you done that you consider to be exceptional in your life? How did you feel?

_____

_____

_____

_____

_____

_____

_____

_____

_____

_____

_____

Begin with the end in mind
The End is the Beginning

As the camera panned each persons face,
Not a dry eye did exist.
Yet on each face a smile spoke
Of contentment, love and bliss.

They came today to honor,
A man who meant so much.
Who gave to all he came to know
And excuse was not his crutch.

He was a man of passion,
Adventure he did exude.
He loved his family and his God,
Until the day they did conclude.

He traveled through the world we know,
Treating all he came to meet
As if each one was someone great
Who could make his life complete.

He touched their lives in many ways,
Each encounter was unique.
He chose to believe that his fellow man,
Was strong and great, not weak.

He chose each day to stretch beyond
The dreams of common man.
He knew that greatness was within his reach,
And that he was in command.

The love he held for his wife and son
Was well beyond belief.
Each day he praised and expressed his love,
So at death there'd be no grief.

He chose to lead by serving,
Giving hope and praise to all.
So we're here today to celebrate
His answer to God's last call.

"To be what we are and to become what we are capable of becoming, is the only creed of life.

-Robert Louis Stevenson

~ ~ ~ ~

Write down any thoughts you may have regarding the poem or the quote.

_____

_____

_____

_____

_____

_____

_____

_____

_____

_____

_____

What do you want people to say about YOU at the end of your life?

_____

_____

_____

_____

_____

_____

_____

_____

_____

_____

_____

Architect of Dreams

I once had a vision, to create and design,
Structures of grandeur that were truly sublime.
I once had a vision, that in my life I would build,
Structures of such beauty, tears would be spilled.

I never was educated in physics or math,
Others suggested I choose a new path.
One day I awoke and my dream it was dead,
Convinced by the world to do something else instead.

But deep in my heart, my passion it grew,
Throughout the years it simmered and brewed.
My passion lay dormant then one day it awoke,
People had told me, my vision was no joke.

Today I have achieved my vision it seems,
I follow a path, as an Architect of Dreams.
I'm an Architect of Dreams, not of steel, brick and stone,
As a builder of men, dreams and visions I hone.

"Go confidently in the direction of your dreams. Live the life you have imagined."

-Henry David Thoreau

~ ~ ~ ~

Write down any thoughts you may have regarding the poem or the quote.

_____
_____
_____
_____
_____
_____
_____
_____
_____
_____

What do you hope to create in your lifetime?

_____
_____
_____
_____
_____
_____
_____
_____
_____
_____

A Vision

I have a vision for a life that I hold
One that's exciting and exceptionally bold.
Healthy and wealthy, adventurous and wise
That is the life for which I now strive.

No one is better than me can't you see.
I am unique, God made only one me.
I have a vision for life that I hold
The plan's been established, I created a mold.

Just follow these steps and soon you will see
That God has created us all to be free.
I have a vision for life that I hold
I share it with you, let your story be told.

"Success is based on imagination plus ambition and the will to work."
-Thomas Edison

~ ~ ~ ~

Write down any thoughts you may have regarding the poem or the quote.

_____

_____

_____

_____

_____

_____

_____

_____

_____

_____

_____

_____

What visions do you hold for your life?

_____

_____

_____

_____

_____

_____

_____

_____

_____

_____

_____

Beyond the Horizon

Look beyond the horizon,
Tell me, what do you see?
Just a fine line on the ocean,
Or a chance to be free?

Beyond the horizon,
That is where I do venture.
Learning about people
On an exotic adventure.

Traveling the world,
Exploring mysterious lands,
The great Caribbean Ocean,
And hot African sands.

The world is my playground,
I tell myself so.
The challenge I have,
Is just where should I go?

Maybe to Europe,
Or the South China Sea.
Diving the Caymans,
God it's great to be free!

Beyond the horizon,
There are no limitations.
The world is my playground,
Fed by my imagination.

"Every noble work is at first impossible."

-Thomas Carlyle

~ ~ ~ ~

Write down any thoughts you may have regarding the poem or the quote.

_____

_____

_____

_____

_____

_____

_____

_____

_____

_____

Where would you like to travel to in the next 12 months? How can it become a reality?

_____

_____

_____

_____

_____

_____

_____

_____

_____

_____

_____

We All Can Fly

The north wind made the Vikings,
So the old saying goes.
Its life's challenges which we face,
That truly make us all grow.

Each man alive truly can fly
When we decide that we really can.
The Wright Brothers, knew they could fly,
They simply believed and mastered a plan.

How many times
Did they crash and burn,
Before they accomplished
What the world called absurd.

How many times
Did Edison fail?
How many times,
Before he prevailed?

Edison decided,
That he really could fly.
Now we have light,
To read our books by.

How often were they laughed at?
Told they were crazy as a loon.
Yet today we have electric light,
And men walking on the moon!

Men of vision always will fail,
But they know when they do.
They review all their actions,
Adjust the plan and just begin anew.

"Where there is no vision the people perish"

-Proverbs 29:18

~ ~ ~ ~

Write down any thoughts you may have regarding the poem or the quote.

_____

_____

_____

_____

_____

_____

_____

_____

_____

_____

What failures have you had? What lessons did you learn?

_____

_____

_____

_____

_____

_____

_____

_____

_____

_____

Dare to Dream

Life is a series of little decisions,
Guided by purpose, enthusiasm and visions.
"Dare to dream!" The little voice screamed.
It's not as hard as it might have seemed.

Life's too short to sit and survive
Dare to dream, take action and thrive.
God created man to prosper and flourish.
Dare to dream and you will be nourished.

How big a goal can you conceive?
Dare to dream, act and achieve.
Roadblocks and obstacles in life you will find,
Dare to dream and improve your mind.

On life's journey toward the ultimate end,
Dare to dream and invite a friend.
Share your vision with one and all
"Dare to dream!" will be your call.

Passion, zeal, zest and vision,
Dare to dream, it's only a decision.
A life of significance, excitement and fun,
Dare to dream, success it will come.

"Cherish your visions and your dreams as they are the children of your soul; the blueprints of your ultimate achievements."

-Napoleon Hill

~ ~ ~ ~

Write down any thoughts you may have regarding the poem or the quote.

_____

_____

_____

_____

_____

_____

_____

_____

_____

What are some of your BIG goals that you want to achieve in your lifetime?

_____

_____

_____

_____

_____

_____

_____

_____

_____

Free to be Dreamers

Now is the time for passion and zeal!
Don't be complacent, asleep at the wheel.
The whole world is moving, don't sit or stand still.
Go out and take action, procrastination you must kill.

The world it is changing, each of us must decide
What world will we live in, where will we reside.
Will you choose the new world, one you help to create?
Or reside in the past, full of anger and hate?

I believe in mankind, naïve that might be.
But without this belief, what world will we see?
We all must seek wisdom, to create and design,
A life that was given by God that's divine.

I have the faith, that in my life I will see,
A world that is peaceful and all men are free.
Free to be dreamers and lifetime achievers,
Compassionate people and righteous believers.

My dream will come true, my quest will succeed.
So daily I choose to step up and to lead.
Lead by example, to give and to serve,
A world that is changing, so each voice can be heard.

"Choice! The key is choice. You have options. You need not spend your life wallowing in failure, ignorance, grief, poverty, shame, and self-pity! There is a better way to live!"

-Og Mandino

~ ~ ~ ~

Write down any thoughts you may have regarding the poem or the quote.

_____

_____

_____

_____

_____

_____

_____

_____

_____

_____

What are your perceptions of the world?

_____

_____

_____

_____

_____

_____

_____

_____

_____

_____

Get a Dream

You ride life,
Or it rides you!
It's really very simple,
You decide and then you do.

Dream the impossible,
All things are possible.
It's all up to you,
Because you are responsible.

You say you've got no dream.
Well, you're really not living.
You're just here for a time,
Simply existing and visiting.

Most of all men,
I am convinced,
Have no vision or dream,
And lack confidence.

Great men of vision,
At one time have all failed.
All still believed
And eventually prevailed.

Without belief,
You're doomed in this life.
To constant anguish and suffering,
Turmoil and strife.

Where there is no vision,
People surely will perish.
So get a big dream,
Your life you will cherish.

"I learned this, at least, by my experience; that if one advances confidently in the direction of his dreams and endeavors to live the life which he has imagined, he will meet with success unexpected in common hours."
-Henry David Thoreau, Walden

~ ~ ~ ~

Write down any thoughts you may have regarding the poem or the quote.

_____

_____

_____

_____

_____

_____

_____

_____

_____

_____

_____

Who do you admire and consider to be men or women of vision?

_____

_____

_____

_____

_____

_____

_____

_____

_____

_____

Get a Vision

I once had a vision, where it went I can't say,
But I woke up one morning, and it had faded away.
Where did it go? It was brilliant and grand.
I dove with the fish, and traveled the land.

The home of a dreamer, I actually built.
High on a hill, I had made it I felt.
I walked by a photo of where I had been,
Stopped right in my tracks, and said, "Oh what a sin!"

What I'd become, was certainly not me.
I was born for adventure, and freedom you see!
I collected my visions, my dreams to succeed,
Went searching for something that could help me achieve.

Today, I'm a dreamer, with a passion for life.
Have a wonderful son, and a fabulous wife!
If you know where you're at, and it's not at the top,
Get a vision, a dream, and don't ever stop.

"I am bigger than anything that can happen to me. All these things, sorrow, misfortune, and suffering, are outside my door. I am in the house and I have the key."

-Charles Fletcher Lummis

~ ~ ~ ~

Write down any thoughts you may have regarding the poem or the quote.

_____

_____

_____

_____

_____

_____

_____

_____

_____

_____

What vision if you achieved it would make you feel fulfilled?

_____

_____

_____

_____

_____

_____

_____

_____

_____

Go Around Once

We go around once,
In this world we are told.
What visions and dreams,
For your life do you hold?

We're designed by The Creator,
So create we all can.
I choose adventure and excitement,
It's all how you plan.

Enthusiasm and passion,
It's just how you feel.
I control my emotions,
and it soon becomes real.

The alternative option,
Is really not thrilling.
I've tried it before,
And I'm no longer willing.

We go around once,
So why not just feel
A life of fulfillment,
Passion and zeal.

Believe it, achieve it!
Just go out and do.
We go around once,
It's all up to you!

"Man is made or unmade by himself. By the right choice he ascends. As a being of power, intelligence, and love, and the lord of his own thoughts, He holds the key to every situation."

-James Allen

~ ~ ~ ~

Write down any thoughts you may have regarding the poem or the quote.

_____

_____

_____

_____

_____

_____

_____

_____

_____

_____

What area of your life are you most passionate about? Area you are least passionate?

_____

_____

_____

_____

_____

_____

_____

_____

_____

_____

Hot Dog or Wienie?

"Hot Dog or Wienie?" I heard the man say.
Which do you choose on this glorious day?

A life of adventure, excitement and fun,
Or spending your days tucked into a bun?

"Hot Dog or Wienie?" the man did repeat!
"Make a decision don't sit on your seat!"

The life of a Hot Dog is glorious and grand.
If you'll develop a vision, a goal and a plan.

The life of a Wienie, seeks to be secure and safe,
Leading a life of going no place!

"Hot Dog or Wienie?" the man he did yell.
"Which do you choose? Oh please won't you tell?"

A Hot Dog will stumble, slip and will fail.
Be willing to risk and eventually prevail.

Living a life of fulfillment and dreams,
While a Wienie gets bitten, complains and just screams!

"Hot Dog or Wienie, how do you vote?"
"A life of excitement or just staying afloat?"

"Hot Dog or Wienie?" The man said again…
"Hot Dog!" I screamed…
"Let the adventure begin!"

"I say to you today, my friends, that in spite of the difficulties
and frustrations of the moment, I still have a dream."
-Martin Luther King Jr.

~ ~ ~ ~

Write down any thoughts you may have regarding the poem or the quote.

_____

_____

_____

_____

_____

_____

_____

_____

_____

_____

What does it mean to you to be a Hot Dog? A Wienie?

_____

_____

_____

_____

_____

_____

_____

_____

_____

_____

_____

I Have a Dream

"I have a dream!"
Dr. King did proclaim.
A vision for freedom,
That for all man is ordained.

A man with a vision,
A dream for mankind
Can create a new world,
Giving sight to the blind!

"I have a dream!"
Has become my new shout.
Showing the world,
What my life's all about.

Yes, there will be challenges,
And, not all will believe.
But, my vision is focused,
On what I can achieve.

To be a big dreamer,
Is a quest all should seek.
God made us to prosper,
Not to be weak.

So at the top of your voice,
Shout, "I have a dream!"
And see what adventures,
Life surely will bring.

"If you do not change your direction, you will end up exactly where you are headed."

-Ancient Chinese Proverb

~ ~ ~ ~

Write down any thoughts you may have regarding the poem or the quote.

_____

_____

_____

_____

_____

_____

_____

_____

_____

_____

What are your thoughts on Martin Luther King Jr. speech?

_____

_____

_____

_____

_____

_____

_____

_____

_____

_____

_____

_____

I'm in Command

My goal was a mountain, thought impossible to climb.
But I knew I could do it, one step at a time.

I first had a vision, a dream you might say.
That life was a game, and in it I'd play.

I would sail on the oceans, explore rivers and streams.
Swim with the dolphins, pursuing my dreams.

My life's an adventure! I tell myself so.
I'm willing to risk, stretch and to grow.

To achieve all my dreams, required a plan.
It's written and specific, now I'm in command.

"I have no fear of the future. Let us go forward into its mysteries, let us tear aside the veils which hide it from our eyes and let us move onward with confidence and courage."

-Winston Churchill

~ ~ ~ ~

Write down any thoughts you may have regarding the poem or the quote.

_____

_____

_____

_____

_____

_____

_____

_____

_____

_____

What mountains have you had to overcome in your life? How did you overcome them?

_____

_____

_____

_____

_____

_____

_____

_____

_____

Life

Debate it, create it, it really won't care.
It's coming and going and not always fair.

How do you perceive it, is really the key.
Suffering and sorrow, or living it free.

How do you design it, is all up to you.
Adventure and passion, or be a me too.

Excitement with purpose, zest and true zeal,
Create it and live it, what a wonderful feel.

How to achieve it, requires a plan.
A step by step process, oh I know that you can.

So, what is the, "It" that only you can create?
It is a life that's worth living, exciting and great!

"The heights of great men reached and kept, were not attained by sudden flight, but they, while their companions slept, were toiling upwards in the night."

-Winston Churchill

~ ~ ~ ~

Write down any thoughts you may have regarding the poem or the quote.

_____

_____

_____

_____

_____

_____

_____

_____

_____

_____

_____

_____

What do you plan to create in the next 12 months?

_____

_____

_____

_____

_____

_____

_____

_____

_____

_____

_____

Now is the Time

Now is the time,
To design a new life.
A son or a daughter,
A husband or wife.

Now is the time,
To create a new you.
Learn to play jazz,
Or rhythm and blues.

Now is the time,
To be a dreamer of dreams.
Have a vision of purpose,
Accomplish great things.

Now is the time,
Why sit and wait?
Get off your duff,
Go out and create.

"What we think or what we believe is, in the end of little consequence. The only thing of consequence is what we do."

-John Ruskin

~ ~ ~ ~

Write down any thoughts you may have regarding the poem or the quote.

_____

_____

_____

_____

_____

_____

_____

_____

_____

_____

How can you re-design your life? Be bold! Dream BIG! Set no limits on your design.

_____

_____

_____

_____

_____

_____

_____

_____

_____

_____

Purpose

What purpose in life,
And beliefs do you hold?
Answer these questions,
Live a life that is bold.

A life with a purpose,
Creates a path that is clear.
Reducing the obstacles,
Turmoil and fear.

Be an "On Purpose Person,"
And you always will know
If the direction you're heading
Is the right way to go.

Defining your purpose
Beliefs and your goals,
Creates a life that is lived,
Full of passions untold.

Take purpose and passion,
Mix in an adventurous dream.
Be willing to act,
And you've got a life that's a scream!

"You have been given the gift of dreams, so dream BIG! Be bold and adventurous."

-Greg Drolet

~ ~ ~ ~

Write down any thoughts you may have regarding the poem or the quote.

_____

_____

_____

_____

_____

_____

_____

_____

_____

_____

What would you do if you knew you could not fail?

_____

_____

_____

_____

_____

_____

_____

_____

_____

_____

_____

The Price

Pay the price for your dream!
Pay the price for your dream!
The words jumped off the page,
And at me did scream.

One out of a hundred,
Will succeed in this quest.
Pay the price for your dreams,
And always do your best.

There is no free lunch!
No matter what you might hear.
Success only comes,
When you work through your fear.

"We are all worms, but I intend to be a glowworm."
-Winston Churchill

~ ~ ~ ~

Write down any thoughts you may have regarding the poem or the quote.

_____

_____

_____

_____

_____

_____

_____

_____

_____

_____

What price will you have to pay for your dream?

_____

_____

_____

_____

_____

_____

_____

_____

_____

_____

Choice

We come into this world,
On the choice of another.
Each with a father,
As well as a mother.

Once we are here,
The fun does begin.
We have the choice,
To lose or to win.

Some people say,
That to this spot we're assigned
Given the choice
And a life to design.

Assigned to a time
With people whom to relate
Given the choice
To love or to hate.

We're here I believe,
As a grand master plan.
To impact the world
And the lives of all man.

How we affect them,
Is the path that we take.
Free will we've been given,
With the choices we make.

"I want to be thoroughly used up when I die, for the harder I work, the more I live. Life is not a brief candle for me. It is a sort of splendid torch which I have got hold of for a moment, and I want to make it burn as brightly as possible before handing it on to future generations."
-George Bernard Shaw

~ ~ ~ ~

Write down any thoughts you may have regarding the poem or the quote.

_____

_____

_____

_____

_____

_____

_____

_____

_____

_____

What impact do you want to make in your world?

_____

_____

_____

_____

_____

_____

_____

_____

_____

_____

I Believe

I believe that I can,
Not that I might.
I believe that I can,
And I'm willing to fight.

I believe that life,
Is to be lived and enjoyed.
That I'll never achieve this,
By being employed.

I believe…
That God made us to win.
That all dreams are possible,
If we'll only begin.

I believe…
In myself and my quest.
That I was born to succeed,
If I just do my best.

I believe…
That I cannot fail.
I learned lessons by stumbling,
And I always prevail.

I believe…
That my purpose in life,
Is to take charge of me,
And design my own life.

"...he allowed himself to be swayed by his conviction that human beings are not born once and for all on the day their mothers give birth to them, but that life obliges them over and over and again to give birth to themselves."
-Gabriel Garcia Marquez, *Love in the Time of Cholera*

~ ~ ~ ~

Write down any thoughts you may have regarding the poem or the quote.

_____

_____

_____

_____

_____

_____

_____

_____

_____

_____

_____

What beliefs do you have about yourself?

_____

_____

_____

_____

_____

_____

_____

_____

_____

_____

I Found Myself Running

I found myself running, running for my life.
Looking over my shoulder, at struggle, anguish and strife.
I found myself looking, in the mirror to the rear,
Focusing on the problems, failures, doubts and fear.

Then one day it hit me, I was living in the past.
Missing all that lie ahead, seeing only what I had passed.
So I forced myself to focus, on the life that lie ahead.
A life I live with passion, not anger, fear and dread.

Today I see my failures, as teachers who can provide,
The answers to my future, and with whom I can reside.
The chaos that is in my life, is opportunity in disguise.
Providing a life of abundance, happiness in unlimited supply.

So each day I seek adventure, not afraid to take a risk.
Because I know that all my failures, lead to harmony and bliss.
Today I go out and do things, living a life beyond compare,
All because I chose to do, what others will not dare.

"Adversity calls forth the soul's courage to bear unflinchingly whatever Heaven sends"

-Euripides

~ ~ ~ ~

Write down any thoughts you may have regarding the poem or the quote.

_____

_____

_____

_____

_____

_____

_____

_____

_____

_____

If you knew you could not fail, what risks would you be willing to take?

_____

_____

_____

_____

_____

_____

_____

_____

_____

_____

Life's Golden Riddle

Working too much,
Living too little,
How to reverse it,
Is life's golden riddle.

Too much time spent impressing,
Not enough time to inspire,
You have time to reverse it,
Before you expire.

It's time to design,
The life of your dreams.
Living beyond,
What a normal life brings.

It's time to stand up,
And recapture your vision!
It will be easy to do,
You just make the decision.

It's time to decide,
That action's required.
Whether you've received a promotion,
Or were recently fired.

It's time to create,
A new life, a new you.
Time to let others see
Just what you can do.

It's time to discard,
A life that's mundane.
Living in mediocrity,
Is simply profane.

"The world breaks every one of us and afterward many are stronger at the broken pieces."

-Ernest Hemingway

~ ~ ~ ~

Write down any thoughts you may have regarding the poem or the quote.

_____

_____

_____

_____

_____

_____

_____

_____

_____

What area of your life, if you focus on improving it, will have the biggest impact? Why?

_____

_____

_____

_____

_____

_____

_____

_____

_____

_____

Old Man Opportunity

Old Man Opportunity,
Is a knockin' at my door.
Been trippin' over dollars,
Picking pennies off the floor.

The Old Man's been a knockin'
But I just can't seem to hear.
Been doing what they told me,
But success ain't gettin' near.

Headed off to college,
Got my sheepskin like they said,
If I keep doin' what I'm doin'
I'll be broke and nearly dead.

But somewhere in the subconscious mind,
The Old Man is always there,
Tellin' me to change my ways,
Take a risk or take a dare.

Old Man Opportunity,
Is a knockin' at my door.
I think this time I'll answer it,
And pick the dollars off the floor.

"On the surface, I am an average person, but to my heart, I am a great moment. The challenge I face is how to dedicate everything I have inside of me to fulfilling this moment."

-Abraham Heschel

~ ~ ~ ~

Write down any thoughts you may have regarding the poem or the quote.

_____

_____

_____

_____

_____

_____

_____

_____

_____

_____

What opportunity is knocking at your door right now? Are you prepared to answer it?

_____

_____

_____

_____

_____

_____

_____

_____

_____

_____

The Masterpiece

They supplied me with the canvas,
The colors and a brush.
Set them on an easel,
Out of the room they quickly rushed.

I stared at a massive void,
The emptiness I did see.
Realizing that the design,
Was completely up to me.

What was the subject of my art?
Which colors would I use?
The patterns that I did paint,
Would be the ones that I would choose.

The tools lay before me,
They all had been supplied.
Would I create a masterpiece?
Or a work that was despised?

As I viewed the pallet,
My eyes danced as they did feast.
Upon all the colors I could choose,
To paint life's masterpiece.

"You can't be great at something unless you're willing to keep falling on your face."

-Cybil Shephard

~ ~ ~ ~

Write down any thoughts you may have regarding the poem or the quote.

_____

_____

_____

_____

_____

_____

_____

_____

_____

_____

_____

How will you paint your life's masterpiece?

_____

_____

_____

_____

_____

_____

_____

_____

_____

_____

_____

You Can't Stay the Same

With every tick of the clock,
We are either growing or dying.
The question you should ponder,
Is, of the two, which are you vying.

No matter how loud,
You may scream and complain,
Try as you may,
You just can't stay the same.

An old Chinese proverb says,
That which is flexible and flowing,
Is healthy and is pliable
Living, strong and growing.

That which is stagnant
Is rigid and surely dying.
So the question to ponder,
Is "Are you living or are you dying?"

What would you choose to become,
If you knew you could not fail?
What would you choose to do,
If you knew you would prevail?

So get excited about your life,
About new sights and sounds!
Find the child that's within you,
Let your energy abound.

Chose to re-invent and remodel,
To revitalize your brain,
Just remember, in this life
You just can't stay the same!

"With life so short, why is the craft of living so long to learn?"

-Chaucer

~ ~ ~ ~

Write down any thoughts you may have regarding the poem or the quote.

_____

_____

_____

_____

_____

_____

_____

_____

_____

_____

_____

What does your inner child look like? What does he / she like to do?

_____

_____

_____

_____

_____

_____

_____

_____

_____

_____

_____

It

The amount has a limit,
A supply that is finite.
You'll never have an excess
So don't bother to fuss or fight.

Try as you might,
It can never be stretched.
It's not flexible or flowing,
It is firmly entrenched.

You receive it at birth,
And in *it* you play.
The it that you are given
Is the gift of just *Today.*

Broken down even further,
Today becomes *Now.*
What you become,
Is the question of *How.*

How will you use *It*?
This wonderful little treat.
Try positive action,
And extraordinary feats!

Today and the *Now,*
Is what life's all about,
Let "Do unto others!"
Become your new shout.

Today and the *Now,*
It is the moment to do.
What you become
Is the life that you choose!

"How many people are trapped in their everyday habits: part numb, part frightened, part indifferent? To have a better life we must keep choosing how we're living."

-Albert Einstein

~ ~ ~ ~

Write down any thoughts you may have regarding the poem or the quote.

_____

_____

_____

_____

_____

_____

_____

_____

_____

_____

_____

What do you know you need to do TODAY, NOW?

_____

_____

_____

_____

_____

_____

_____

_____

_____

_____

_____

The Journey

I found myself on a journey, attempting to find the why.
The answers always eluded me, no matter how long I'd try.
The journey on which I travelled, was one of seeking out,
What lessons that we were born to learn, of the pain that shouted out.

The suffering of a woman's life, what lessons were we to learn?
The answers just eluded me, the lessons I could not discern.
Then one day while I sat and read, I began to slowly suspect,
That the road that I was traveling on, was the journey of introspect.

"Independent of others and in concert with others, your main task in life is to do what you can best do and become what you can potentially be."

-Erich Fromm

~ ~ ~ ~

Write down any thoughts you may have regarding the poem or the quote.

_____

_____

_____

_____

_____

_____

_____

_____

_____

_____

What lessons have you learned from your challenges in life? How have you grown?

_____

_____

_____

_____

_____

_____

_____

_____

_____

The Enemy

Attack the enemy,
You know where he lies!
You know that you should,
But simply won't try.

Attack the enemy,
Or he'll kill you for sure.
It won't be easy,
But actions the cure.

Attack the enemy,
Before it's too late.
He's not advancing,
He's decided to wait.

I decided to attack,
Because I now see,
That the enemy I'm battling,
Is really inside of me.

"There is no passion to be found playing small—in settling for a life that is less than the one you are capable of living."

-Nelson Mandela

~ ~ ~ ~

Write down any thoughts you may have regarding the poem or the quote.

_____

_____

_____

_____

_____

_____

_____

_____

_____

_____

What is the internal enemy that has been holding you back?

_____

_____

_____

_____

_____

_____

_____

_____

_____

_____

Significance

A life of significance
Is what I perceive,
As my purpose in life
And what I believe.

How to create it,
Is the challenge I see.
So I keep my focus and dream,
And I know it will be.

To do something significant,
I must stick out my neck.
Be willing to risk, cross the line,
Say, "What the heck!"

Change is inevitable,
Personal growth is an option.
Choosing the latter,
Makes me truly unstoppable.

A life of significance,
Is a matter of choice.
Take the action required,
And in life you will rejoice.

Get on with the job,
Teach the world to create.
With a vision and passion,
It's never too late.

To some this sounds silly,
Hokey and trite.
But I'm living my purpose,
And I know that I'm right!

"As for me, I know nothing else but miracles."
                                        -Walt Whitman

~ ~ ~ ~

Write down any thoughts you may have regarding the poem or the quote.

_____

_____

_____

_____

_____

_____

_____

_____

_____

_____

How would you define your purpose in life?

_____

_____

_____

_____

_____

_____

_____

_____

_____

_____

Thank You

They gave me a vision
That I could succeed.
All dreams are possible,
If I only believed.

Never once as I grew,
Did I hear that I couldn't.
Would not have believed it,
'Cause I knew that I shouldn't.

They taught me the lessons,
Of love and respect.
To do more for others,
Than they might expect.

They gave me a vision,
That in God, I should seek,
The blessings of life,
And to always be meek.

Thank you dear Father,
As I say this little prayer,
For a mother and father,
That always were there.

"The most difficult thing is the decision to act, the rest is just tenacity."
-Amelia Earhart

~ ~ ~ ~

Write down any thoughts you may have regarding the poem or the quote.

_____

_____

_____

_____

_____

_____

_____

_____

_____

_____

_____

What lessons did you learn from your parents?

_____

_____

_____

_____

_____

_____

_____

_____

_____

_____

_____

Lead by Example

We can guide by example,
Pick them up when they fall.
Love them and hug them,
And help them stand tall.

Teach them about honesty,
Integrity and love,
About morals and values,
And "The Man" up above.

We must lead by example,
If we want them to believe.
Life's about leading,
If you want to succeed.

Our children need heroes,
Who can lead and then teach,
That life's an adventure,
If you're willing to reach.

They must know you are human,
And, yes, you have failed.
Made mistakes, said, "I'm sorry,"
And eventually prevailed.

Lead by example,
Do what you say!
Your children will love you,
They will lead the same way.

"With all your science can you tell me how it is, and when it is, that light comes into the soul?"

-Henry David Thoreau

~ ~ ~ ~

Write down any thoughts you may have regarding the poem or the quote.

_____

_____

_____

_____

_____

_____

_____

_____

_____

_____

How can you lead by example in your life?

_____

_____

_____

_____

_____

_____

_____

_____

_____

_____

I Love You

"I love you," I whispered.
"Thank you," she said.
In living and dying,
These words must be said.

"I love you," I whispered.
"I love you," she did reply.
It's love and respect,
On which we all must rely.

It's not always easy,
To keep this in perspective.
But, continue to try,
And make it your objective.

"I love you, I love you,
And thanks for the hugs,
When I brought in the beetles,
The spiders and bugs."

"I love you Mom,"
I said with a tear.
You gave me so much,
At a cost that was dear.

"I love you son!"
What greater words said.
With a caress on the cheek,
And a pat on the head.

"To be yourself in a world that is constantly trying to make you something else is the greatest accomplishment"

-Ralph Waldo Emerson

~ ~ ~ ~

Write down any thoughts you may have regarding the poem or the quote.

_____

_____

_____

_____

_____

_____

_____

_____

_____

_____

What are some of your great memories with your Mom?

_____

_____

_____

_____

_____

_____

_____

_____

_____

_____

Going Home

Each time that we would visit,
Or talk upon the phone,
The conversation always ended,
"I am going home."

Yes, no matter where we travel,
Or places that we roam,
The roads in life lead to one place,
That destination's…Home.

"Be creative. Use unconventional thinking. And have the guts to carry it out."
-Lee Iacocca

~ ~ ~ ~

Write down any thoughts you may have regarding the poem or the quote.

_____

_____

_____

_____

_____

_____

_____

_____

_____

_____

Who has gone "Home" that you wish you had more time with? Why?

_____

_____

_____

_____

_____

_____

_____

_____

_____

_____

_____

_____

A Beauty to Behold

I met her many years ago,
To this day the memory's sweet.
Her beautiful eyes and golden hair,
With a smile that is so sweet.

She is a beauty to behold,
The treasure I had sought.
For many years I searched the land,
The vision I now had caught.

We traveled throughout this great big world,
Seeking adventure in our lives.
Doing all the things others just read about,
Not willing to just survive!

She taught me to communicate,
To truly appreciate what I possess.
I learned to read in a different way,
And to see the meaning of true success.

Integrity, love and honesty,
Are the values that she holds.
My love for her will never die,
She's my beauty, even as we both grow old.

"Give the world the best you have and the best will come back to you"
-Myrna Ericksen

~ ~ ~ ~

Write down any thoughts you may have regarding the poem or the quote.

_____

_____

_____

_____

_____

_____

_____

_____

_____

_____

Who is the most beautiful person you know? Why?

_____

_____

_____

_____

_____

_____

_____

_____

_____

_____

Snuggle Buddy

He came to us in September,
Our little bundle of joy.
He's growing now into manhood,
No longer a little boy.

He's creative and he's handsome,
And simply a whole lot of fun.
Never thought about having two,
Cause he's our number one.

In his mission in life,
We know he'll go far.
Whether it's changing the world,
Or playing guitar.

I love to hear his laughter,
His impressions and his smile.
I love to be with him,
He's still mine for awhile.

The gifts that I can give him,
Are wisdom, truth and hugs.
He's my little snuggle buddy,
The son I truly love.

"Most obstacles melt away when we make up our minds to boldly walk through them."

-Orison Swett Marden

~ ~ ~ ~

Write down any thoughts you may have regarding the poem or the quote.

_____

_____

_____

_____

_____

_____

_____

_____

_____

_____

Who in your life is your true love? Why?

_____

_____

_____

_____

_____

_____

_____

_____

_____

_____

_____

A Father and Son's Adventure

Crusin' down Coast Highway looking for a place to stay,
Exploring life's opportunities from L.A. to Monterey.

Been lookin' for adventures ever since my life begun,
Now at last I have the chance to share it with my son.

Life it is an adventure or so I've heard it said.
We're on this journey that's called life, someday we will be dead.

So why on earth, I ask you, don't we grab it by the tail
Riding life for all it's worth, blazing new and exciting trails.

Exploring old San Simeon, camping at Kirk Creek,
Traveling up and down the coast, been gone for 'bout a week.

Many travelers will pass this way but never really see,
All the nature God created, the mountains, flowers and trees.

Crusin' north on Highway 1, just a father and a son,
This is what life's about, adventures, love and fun.

Winding along Highway 1 the road does twist and turn.
Never knowin' just what lies ahead, and excitement in us burns.

A taste for adventure is in our blood, we're seeking rainbows in the sky.
Wondering what the next turn will bring, perhaps whales passing by.

Perhaps we'll see a condor, one of California's greatest birds,
Or a waterfall settling on a beach, its beauty beyond all words.

"The highest form of ignorance is when you reject something you know nothing about."

-Wayne Dyer

~ ~ ~ ~

Write down any thoughts you may have regarding the poem or the quote.

_____

_____

_____

_____

_____

_____

_____

_____

_____

_____

_____

What great adventure do you want to go on? What would you do?

_____

_____

_____

_____

_____

_____

_____

_____

_____

_____

_____

A Father's Lament

I have all this wisdom,
A good life I have lived.
But no one's willing to ask me,
About what's inside my head.

I have all of this wisdom,
Now tell me, what do I do?
No one seems to be asking,
Oh, what should I do?

I've lived all these years,
And acquired so much knowledge.
But, no one is asking,
You see, they all have gone to college.

I also have gone to school
The College of Hard Knocks,
Done manual labor to feed the kids,
In the freight yards and on the docks.

I've lived through the Great Depression,
The horrors of the Great War.
I have all of this wisdom,
Now tell me, what's it for?

I fought for this country's freedom,
Accomplished many hard tasks
I have all of this wisdom,
It's yours if you'll only ask!

"I shall allow no man to belittle my soul by making me hate him."
                                                    -Booker T. Washington

~ ~ ~ ~

Write down any thoughts you may have regarding the poem or the quote.

_____

_____

_____

_____

_____

_____

_____

_____

_____

_____

What wisdom did you receive from your father that has helped you in life?

_____

_____

_____

_____

_____

_____

_____

_____

_____

_____

Up On the Roof

My grandpa loved music,
Was a joker and loved a spoof.
Heard me play the guitar,
Asked, "Can you play on the roof?"

I told him, "Sorry grandpa,"
"I don't know that one yet,"
"But I'll see if I can learn it,
So grandpa don't you fret."

I asked if he knew,
Who wrote the old tune?
He looked at me and smiled,
Said, "Let's watch a cartoon."

For years I did search,
Music stores near and far.
I looked in California,
In Tibet and Zanzibar.

I thought it might be a classic,
Maybe jazz or the blues.
I scoured the brass,
Violins and kazoos.

No matter where I looked,
I could never find,
That silly old tune,
I can't get out of my mind.

So, grandpa, oh grandpa,
I looked for so long,
But, I'm better on the guitar
And I wrote you a song.

It's a song about love,
And a grandpa's great spoof.
About a boy who plays music,
Up on the roof.

"You don't wait for inspiration, you intentionally seek it out. You create your own inspired environment and motivation is your responsibility. After all, it's your life."

-Greg Drolet

~ ~ ~ ~

Write down any thoughts you may have regarding the poem or the quote.

_____

_____

_____

_____

_____

_____

_____

_____

_____

_____

_____

What stories do you have about your grandparents that positively impacted you?

_____

_____

_____

_____

_____

_____

_____

_____

_____

_____

The Noble Path

I got a call that early morn,
At first I thought it was a joke.
But, as I watched the scenes unfold,
I knew a new order had been invoked.

The message seen was strong and clear,
Man still did not understand.
To kill and maim in heavens name,
God never did command.

Yes, man's inhumanity to his fellow man,
I'm sad to say is strong.
Even though we're taught The Word,
And this madness is always wrong.

The root of evil in our lives,
Is based in fear and hate.
Terror inflicted on all mankind,
We must eliminate.

Only then will we achieve,
The purpose for which we exist.
To live a life, of abundance and love,
So we really must persist.

Each of us must transcend the hate,
Or suffer God's mighty wrath.
So glorify the righteous way,
And choose the noble path.

"They took away what should have been my eyes, but I remember Milton's Paradise. They took away what should have been my ears, Beethoven came and wiped away my tears. They took away what should have been my tongue, but I had talked to God when I was young. He would not let them take away my soul possessing that, I still possess the whole.

-Helen Keller

~ ~ ~ ~

Write down any thoughts you may have regarding the poem or the quote.

_____

_____

_____

_____

_____

_____

_____

_____

_____

_____

What has been taken from you that you realized later was a blessing?

_____

_____

_____

_____

_____

_____

_____

_____

_____

_____

Strength In the Lord

My strength and my confidence,
Is found in the Lord.
Living life in Jesus' name,
Is what I now move toward.

I embrace the Lord's love,
Live victorious in joy and peace.
Anchored to the Rock of Salvation,
It's to Him that I daily reach.

I am a sinner plain and true,
With frustration, hurts and sorrow.
But, in the loving arms of Jesus,
His strength I may now borrow.

I receive all my energy,
From Almighty God above.
My passion for life and living,
From the One I truly love.

Yes, my strength, my hope, my confidence,
And the purpose I now see.
Comes from the great Lord Jesus,
Who has allowed me to be.

"When you get into a tight place and everything goes against you
'til it seems though you could not hold on a minute longer, never give up then,
for that is just the place and time that the tide will turn.

-Harriet Beecher Stowe

~ ~ ~ ~

Write down any thoughts you may have regarding the poem or the quote.

_____

_____

_____

_____

_____

_____

_____

_____

_____

_____

_____

Where do you find your strength and confidence? Why?

_____

_____

_____

_____

_____

_____

_____

_____

_____

_____

_____

Desolate Roads

I've traveled down desolate roads,
Of driving rains, sleet and snow.
Yet, when I thought it never would end,
A rainbow appeared that God did send.

And so it is, with life it seems,
That we each are faced with challenges unforeseen.
When things are darkest in our days,
God sends a light to show the way.

"Can you walk on water? You have done no better than a straw.
Can you soar in the air? You have done no better than to fly.
Conquer your heart; then you may become somebody."
                              -Ansari of Heart, Persian Philosopher

~ ~ ~ ~

Write down any thoughts you may have regarding the poem or the quote.

_____

_____

_____

_____

_____

_____

_____

_____

_____

_____

What is a dark day or days that you've had and what did you learn?

_____

_____

_____

_____

_____

_____

_____

_____

_____

_____

A Few Thoughts

I travelled along with a flying dragon
Blue and black its wings a waggin'
Ziggin' here and zaggin' there
On the winds of life without a care.

I've travelled along with a pel-i-can
If a bird can fly surely I can!
On a bike or boat or motor car
Traveling with creatures I feel so on par.

Swimming deep beneath the sea
All God's creatures inspire me.
I've dived Aruba and Bonaire
As well as Curacao without a care.

The Cayman Islands shared their treasures
And with each dive life enhanced my pleasures.
I travelled deep into a mountain glen
Saw the great bald eagle and singing wren.

I've hiked the Grand Canyon with tears of joy
While my wife was pregnant with my little boy.
I've journeyed throughout most of the U.S of A
With more land to see and songs to play.

Yes, I've been blessed I must admit
To a life of adventure I still commit.
Life is grand and short as well
These are just a few thoughts I had to tell.

"One of the greatest gifts you can give to anyone is the gift of attention."
-Jim Rohn

~ ~ ~ ~

Write down any thoughts you may have regarding the poem or the quote.

_____

_____

_____

_____

_____

_____

_____

_____

_____

_____

What dreams have you lost that need to be rekindled?

_____

_____

_____

_____

_____

_____

_____

_____

_____

_____

I Am Unique

I have a talent, I am unique.
What I achieve is what I in fact speak.
I am unique, just like everyone else.
What I become, is what I say to myself.

God's given talent, is to go out and create.
In so many ways, he allows me to be great.
Now what I do with it, is all up to me,
God's there to guide us not to do it you see.

So when the urge to create takes me by the hand,
I'm grateful you see, because I know He's in command.
These talents I'm given, are special I know,
And I thank God above, for the gift He's bestowed.

The challenge becomes, which way do I use
All the gifts I've been given, and how do I choose?
I guess it's quite easy, one really can't say,
Just offer it up and let God lead the way.

"Beware when the great God lets loose a thinker on this planet."
-Ralph Waldo Emerson

~ ~ ~ ~

Write down any thoughts you may have regarding the poem or the quote.

_____

_____

_____

_____

_____

_____

_____

_____

_____

_____

What talents and strengths do you possess? How are you using them?

_____

_____

_____

_____

_____

_____

_____

_____

_____

_____

A Mission

I have a mission,
To build a fire within
All who are looking,
For a new life to begin.

A fire of passion,
Excitement and zeal
Burning deep inside,
With the power to heal.

A fire so bright,
Alive and so strong.
A spirit ablaze,
Directing all where they belong.

"Nature of men is always the same, it is their habits that separates them."
-Confucius

~ ~ ~ ~

Write down any thoughts you may have regarding the poem or the quote.

_____

_____

_____

_____

_____

_____

_____

_____

_____

_____

_____

What is your perceived mission in life? How will you accomplish it?

_____

_____

_____

_____

_____

_____

_____

_____

_____

_____

_____

A Quiet Giant

Success I have had, and then lost it all.
But through all the pain, I kept answering the call.
The call to provide stewardship, and to start leading the way,
Caring not what others might say.

I've learned to see life through other people's eyes,
By dropping down my own disguise.
Life is not about the look I show,
It's all about the path I go.

A big mouth frog I cannot be,
My life's about integrity.
So a quiet giant I will become,
Leading by example, until the job is done.

"Never look to the ground for your next step.
Greatness belongs to those who look to the horizon."

-Olympic Athletes Motto

~ ~ ~ ~

Write down any thoughts you may have regarding the poem or the quote.

_____

_____

_____

_____

_____

_____

_____

_____

_____

_____

_____

What does it mean to you to be a Quiet Giant?

_____

_____

_____

_____

_____

_____

_____

_____

_____

_____

_____

_____

Actions Speak

I choose to lead by example,
My actions speak louder than words.
To achieve all my dreams,
I cannot follow the herd.

My voice must be heard,
But spoken through my deeds.
Being not boisterous,
It's through actions that I lead.

My actions speak louder,
Than the words that I speak.
Rewards gained by service,
Is the only gift that I seek.

"As long as a man stands in his own way, everything seems to be in his way."
-Ralph Waldo Emerson

~ ~ ~ ~

Write down any thoughts you may have regarding the poem or the quote.

_____

_____

_____

_____

_____

_____

_____

_____

_____

_____

How can you lead more intentionally with your actions?

_____

_____

_____

_____

_____

_____

_____

_____

_____

_____

_____

The Island

I'm searching for that island, void of anger, fear and hate.
A world we can live in, where all people can relate.
I know that island does exist, I've seen it in my mind.
Just how we all get there, is the answer we must find.

The world's about people, how our lives are intertwined,
We must focus on the answer, the island we must find.
The island that we're seeking is found deep within each soul,
The question you must ask yourself, is the journey worth the toll?

The island that we're seeking, is not a place to hide.
But rather it's the island where the answers do reside.
The answers that the island holds, to where do we find peace?
Are found within each one of us, and well within our reach.

The island goes by many names,
And will be found when you demand,
That love and hope replace the hate,
And you serve your fellow man.

"Life is a battle in which we fall from wounds we receive in running away."
-William L. Sullivan

~ ~ ~ ~

Write down any thoughts you may have regarding the poem or the quote.

_____

_____

_____

_____

_____

_____

_____

_____

_____

_____

Where do you find peace? What is special about it?

_____

_____

_____

_____

_____

_____

_____

_____

_____

_____

The Servant

The world now is calling, all men to serve,
The servant you see, is the one that is heard.

Many will sit, waiting to be served,
Rarely, if ever, is their voice really heard.

The world now is seeking, the servant of man,
These are the people who achieve and command.

The server of men, are the one's that can see,
That the world needs servants if we want to be free.

So take off your suit-coat, your hat and your tie,
Put on a apron and give serving a try.

"Do unto others" and see what it brings,
soon you'll discover that greatness will spring.

Become a steward of freedom, commit you will serve,
Life is too short for your voice not to be heard.

"I have learned silence from the talkative, tolerance from the intolerant and kindness from the unkind. I should not be ungrateful to those who teach."
-Kahlil Gibran

~ ~ ~ ~

Write down any thoughts you may have regarding the poem or the quote.

_____

_____

_____

_____

_____

_____

_____

_____

_____

_____

What does servanthood mean to you? Do you apply it in your life? How?

_____

_____

_____

_____

_____

_____

_____

_____

_____

_____

_____

The Teacher

I have a Teacher, a Mentor if you will,
Who walks along with me as I travel life's hills.
Daily I consult on which way I should go,
What I should do and how can I grow?

The Teacher's been with me since before I was born,
Some days He praises and other days He scorns.
The mentor encourages me if I fail or I win,
Guides me on my daily quest and when against Him I sin.

"You can't let business dictate the rhythm of your life; the idea is to fit the job into your life, not your life into the job."

-Michael J. Fox

~ ~ ~ ~

Write down any thoughts you may have regarding the poem or the quote.

_____

_____

_____

_____

_____

_____

_____

_____

_____

_____

Who are your mentors in life?

_____

_____

_____

_____

_____

_____

_____

_____

_____

_____

40/40 Blues

I woke up this morning,
And my feet hit the floor.
Took a nice hot shower,
Now, I'm walkin' out the door.

See I got me the blues,
Yeah, the 40/40 blues.
I never shoulda listened,
But, I'm wearing my working shoes.

Mama told me, "Honey,
Ya gotta go to school.
Get a good education,
Don't be workin' like a fool."

So I went off and got my sheepskin,
My resume and a new suit.
Got on the treadmill called a job,
Man, I was in hot pursuit.

Then I met a gentleman,
Who said, "say, son don't you know?
It's not about trading time for dollars,
It's all about CASHFLOW!"

"Doubt whom you will, but never yourself."

-American Proverb

~ ~ ~ ~

Write down any thoughts you may have regarding the poem or the quote.

_____

_____

_____

_____

_____

_____

_____

_____

_____

_____

_____

How can you improve your financial situation in the next 12 months?

_____

_____

_____

_____

_____

_____

_____

_____

_____

_____

The Heard

I'm not part of the herd!
I'm part of the heard!
Those who have heard,
That the herds not the word.

If you're part of the herd,
Your futures absurd.
But if you follow the heard,
Then your life is secured.

So what you may ask,
Is the heard actually hearing?
Why, they're hearing the lesson of life,
That the herd keep on fearing!

Fearing to lead,
And not follow the herd.
Becoming unique,
So their voice can be heard.

So how you may ask,
Do I follow the heard?
Just make *the* decision,
To *not* follow the herd.

"Success comes in CANS, not in Can't"

-Tommy Lasorda

~ ~ ~ ~

Write down any thoughts you may have regarding the poem or the quote.

_____

_____

_____

_____

_____

_____

_____

_____

_____

_____

_____

If you don't follow the herd, what will your life look like?

_____

_____

_____

_____

_____

_____

_____

_____

_____

_____

Keep on Truckin'

I've been traveling on a path,
Getting where I am today.
Crazy thing about it is,
I doubt I'm going to stay.

Learned all I could to get here,
Yet, I know there's volumes more.
Not really sure what I'll find,
Or what life's got in store.

I do know if I stay here,
The adventure will be incomplete.
So I think I'll keep on truckin'
Expand my mind and move my feet.

So when the journey's over,
It never can be said,
"the poor guy never lived,
So the old coot can't be dead!"

"Too low they build, who build beneath the stars."
-Edward Young, 18th Century English poet

~ ~ ~ ~

Write down any thoughts you may have regarding the poem or the quote.

_____

_____

_____

_____

_____

_____

_____

_____

_____

_____

What skills, lessons, or talents have you acquired that will help you achieve your dreams?

_____

_____

_____

_____

_____

_____

_____

_____

_____

Saturday and Sunday

Six Saturdays and a Sunday, oh wouldn't that be grand?
It really is possible if you develop a plan.

Saturday One, you might visit the lake,
Eating an ice cream, or a big chocolate cake.

Saturday Two, now what can we do?
Go on an African safari or visit the zoo.

Saturday Three, a new adventure begins,
Diving the oceans on a whale shark's fin.

Saturday Four, a great world to be seen.
Maybe have lunch at the *Tavern on the Green.*

Saturday Five, an exploration is sought.
Travel the Caribbean, there are diamonds to be bought.

Saturday Six, oh my, what a treat.
I can live all my dreams and never repeat.

Then it is Sunday, and we thank God for our life,
All we've been given, and our children and wife.

"If you only knock long enough and loud enough at the gate,
you are sure to wake up somebody."

-Longfellow

~ ~ ~ ~

Write down any thoughts you may have regarding the poem or the quote.

_____

_____

_____

_____

_____

_____

_____

_____

_____

_____

How would you spend Six Saturdays and a Sunday each week?

_____

_____

_____

_____

_____

_____

_____

_____

_____

_____

The C.E.O

Who is in charge?
I demand to know!
This is important,
I want the C.E.O.

What do you mean,
You don't know who he is?
Find him young man,
This is serious biz!

Who makes the decisions?
Who makes the calls?
Is there a boss?
Or do you just roam the halls?

You've worked here how long?
You say all of your life?
And still you don't know,
The C.E.O. of your life!

Get with the program!
Get into the game!
Make some decisions!
You can't stay the same!

You're in control,
Through happiness and strife.
You choose the future,
You're the C.E.O. of your life!

"When you change the way you look at things, the things you look at change"
-Dr. Wayne Dyer

~ ~ ~ ~

Write down any thoughts you may have regarding the poem or the quote.

_____

_____

_____

_____

_____

_____

_____

_____

_____

_____

At what point in your life did you realize you were the CEO of your life?
What changed?

_____

_____

_____

_____

_____

_____

_____

_____

_____

_____

_____

Freckles

A tiny little freckle,
A little dot upon my face.
Making me so special,
Unique in the human race.

A funny little freckle,
I found upon my ear.
I wonder how it got there,
And if I have one on my rear?

Sometimes when I am depressed,
And not in a happy spot,
I simply look down at my arm,
And start playing connect the dots.

It really is quite wonderful,
To have these friends so rare.
Each one of them is so cute,
Some even come in pairs.

They often seem like rabbits,
Starting out with only two.
But many times there are hundreds more,
Before the day is through.

A tiny little freckle,
What they do I have no clue.
I'll only start to worry,
If I find them on my shoe.

Silly little freckles,
They really are quite neat.
My little friends they are all over,
From my head down to my feet.

Many people seem to notice them,
And they always bring a smile.
Some people tell me,
They could see them from a mile.

I'm not quite sure how to end this.
It's a silly poem I know.
But, if I'm ever in an avalanche,
Look for freckles in the snow.

"Live full, die empty"
-Les Brown

~ ~ ~ ~

Write down any thoughts you may have regarding the poem or the quote.

_____

_____

_____

_____

_____

_____

_____

_____

_____

_____

Who or what in your life has so inspired you that you would write about them?
Why?

_____

_____

_____

_____

_____

_____

_____

_____

_____

_____

_____

Ears

My daddy he once told me,
God gave most of us just two.
Most of the time however,
Their used by just a few.

They usually come in pairs,
Rarely only just one.
Some people will use them,
Live a life of joy and fun.

They have a strange and unusual name.
Yes, we call them our ears.
Most people see them,
But don't use them to hear.

They think they are attached
As a decorative device.
Used to hang all sorts of things,
To attract and to entice.

If only we would use them,
For their intended use.
We'd live a life of wonderment,
Not sorrow and excuse.

"Live Boldly. Love more, laugh more, grow more and become more."
-Greg Drolet

~ ~ ~ ~

Write down any thoughts you may have regarding the poem or the quote.

_____

_____

_____

_____

_____

_____

_____

_____

_____

_____

_____

How do you think your life would change if you listened more and spoke less?

_____

_____

_____

_____

_____

_____

_____

_____

_____

_____

_____

Me

Throughout my life,
I've had high self-esteem.
Always ambitious,
Pursuing my dream.

There once was a time,
When I was quite a squirrel.
Going through high school,
And learning about girls.

Other than that,
I can honestly say,
There was no one
I faced that I couldn't outplay.

Oh sure there were sports,
That in them I stunk.
But I think only basketball,
'Cause I never could dunk.

"Quality is not an act. It's a habit"

-Tony Robbins

~ ~ ~ ~

Write down any thoughts you may have regarding the poem or the quote.

_____

_____

_____

_____

_____

_____

_____

_____

_____

_____

At what time in your life did you feel the least powerful? How did you respond?

_____

_____

_____

_____

_____

_____

_____

_____

_____

_____

The "Overfat" Blues

What is the key to what we will be?
Well, nutrition and exercise will help set you free.

What good is your money, if you don't have your health?
Design a healthy new life and enjoy all of life's wealth.

Create a plan of action, watching what you daily eat.
Start running, swimming or biking, but get up onto your feet.

Don't be a couch potato, sitting on the old couch.
Get off your lazy duff, don't be an old grouch.

Remember in the past, when you could see your new shoes?
For years now you've been singing, The Overfat Blues.

The Overflat Blues, played in the key of E.
E stands for eating, everything you see.

Just dump all the cerveza, all the chips and all the dips.
You know that it just goes, straight to the old hips.

Break out the nice green broccoli, celery and tofu.
Walk every morning, no more Overfat Blues.

The Overfat Blues are a tune from the past,
Now you just sing of the Lean Muscle Mass.

"What lies behind us and what lies before us,
are small matters compared to what lies within us."
-Ralph Waldo Emerson

~ ~ ~ ~

Write down any thoughts you may have regarding the poem or the quote.

_____

_____

_____

_____

_____

_____

_____

_____

_____

_____

_____

Do you desire a healthier physical lifestyle? What needs to change?

_____

_____

_____

_____

_____

_____

_____

_____

_____

_____

_____

The Healer

We've got a new pill
Designed to help you to win.
This exciting new supplement
Is our confidence building vitamin.

This phenomenal new pill,
Has produced a tremendous reaction.
It's designed to promote growth,
Consistency and action.

This wonderful healer,
Requires no prescription you see.
It's found within you
And is actually free.

It's created for prevention,
And has the power to cure.
All that will ail you
Of this I am sure.

The healer is a smile,
And the guts to just say "Hi!"
Just go out and do it,
Don't tell me you will try!

"You haven't lived until you learn how to give"

-Kirk Douglas

~ ~ ~ ~

Write down any thoughts you may have regarding the poem or the quote.

_____

_____

_____

_____

_____

_____

_____

_____

_____

_____

_____

Who has made a positive impact on you by their smile or positive attitude? How? When?

_____

_____

_____

_____

_____

_____

_____

_____

_____

_____

_____

'T

'T, 'T, why are these words so familiar to me?
Oh yes I remember, I learned them in school
It's a land that's inhabited by stump heads and fools.

The land it was ruled by weakness it seems,
By a king with no vision, ambition or dreams.

The lowly King Can't, believed that he couldn't,
And he told all the stump heads, they shouldn't and wouldn't.

The fools didn't think that they could, so they didn't.
And they taught all their children about wouldn't, can't and couldn't.

The king had a son, Prince Can't and he couldn't,
Believe that life was all about, can't, didn't, wouldn't and shouldn't.

He awoke one great morning and knew something was awry.
He looked at his name and added RY.

Can Try, realized there is only Didn't and Do!
Try is a misnomer, it's fiction, just do.

He traveled his land with a beautiful new feel,
Promoting a life of passion and zeal.

"For imagination sets the goal "picture" which our automatic mechanism works on. We act or fail to act, not because of "will", as is so commonly believed, but because of imagination."

-Maxwell Maltz

~ ~ ~ ~

Write down any thoughts you may have regarding the poem or the quote.

_____

_____

_____

_____

_____

_____

_____

_____

_____

_____

What have you done when you thought you couldn't? How did it turn out?

_____

_____

_____

_____

_____

_____

_____

_____

_____

_____

Expect a Miracle

Expect a miracle! The words ring in my brain,
Or suffer the option of turmoil and pain.

Expect a miracle! Life will be grand.
Just find a mentor and develop a plan.

Expect a miracle! Develop a vision,
Relinquish the fears that hold you in prison.

Expect a miracle! How big can you dream?
It's really much easier than it initially seems.

Expect a miracle! Just go out and do it!
Now is the time, take action, get to it.

Expect a miracle! Create a new you.
Then teach another that yes, they also can to.

Expect a miracle! Learn all that you can.
And your life will be glorious, special and grand.

"When the eagles are silent, the parrots begin to jabber."
-Winston Churchill

~ ~ ~ ~

Write down any thoughts you may have regarding the poem or the quote.

_____

_____

_____

_____

_____

_____

_____

_____

_____

_____

What miracle would you like to see in your life? What difference would it make?

_____

_____

_____

_____

_____

_____

_____

_____

_____

_____

Take Flight

Reach inside of yourself,
And get into the game.
Sharpen your senses,
It'll be impossible not to change.

Begin looking at life,
With a different angle and view.
If everyone is doing it,
Become one of the few.

If the masses go left,
Then why not go right?
If they all sit down,
Decide to take flight.

If you focus on excelling,
While everyone else is competing,
You'll live a life of abundance,
While their success will be fleeting.

*"Ask, and you will receive; seek, and you will find; knock, and
it will be opened unto you."*

-Holy Bible

~ ~ ~ ~

Write down any thoughts you may have regarding the poem or the quote.

_____

_____

_____

_____

_____

_____

_____

_____

_____

_____

What does abundance and excellence mean to you?

_____

_____

_____

_____

_____

_____

_____

_____

_____

_____

Failure

Failing is failure to see that you failed,
Not willing to change, just continuing to flail.
Failing is failure, to see change is a must.
Continuing to complain, anguish and fuss.

If you are where you are, knowing all that you know,
Then you really must change, if there's a new place you want to go.
If you got what you have, doing just what you did,
Then you really must change, if it's a new life that you bid.

To get what you want, you must see where you are
If you're willing to change, in life you'll go far.
If you know what you want, and are willing to change,
Create a new habit that your brain can arrange.

If you're busy being busy, always mopping the floor,
Just turn off the faucet, and try a new door.
If you're busy being busy, in your little rat race,
Be willing to change, you will find a great place.

A place that is full of excitement and joy,
A world full of wonder, you can make it your toy.

"I can't spare this man, he fights."

-Abraham Lincoln
Response to critics requesting the removal of General Grant

~ ~ ~ ~

Write down any thoughts you may have regarding the poem or the quote.

_____

_____

_____

_____

_____

_____

_____

_____

_____

How has failure shaped your life?

_____

_____

_____

_____

_____

_____

_____

_____

_____

_____

Fear and Doubt

Living a life of fear and doubt,
Is not at all what my life's all about.

I embrace fear, as a friend, not as a foe,
And boldly travel, where others won't go.

I fear no one or anything,
And experience the adventure, that only risk brings.

I live a life of fulfillment and dreams,
Conquering the challenges, that life surely brings.

I choose excitement, adventure and freedom,
Seeking the key to God's mighty kingdom.

When I see the twins, called Fear and Doubt,
I focus my dreams and take the high route.

I love rejection, it strengthens my will,
Pushing me forward to dreams I fulfill.

Reject me I love it! No man do I fear!
It's passion that drives me, I'm focused and clear.

Fear and doubt, it's for only the weak,
I'm about passion, it's adventure that I seek.

Living a life of fear and of doubt,
Is not at all what my life's about.

"One can choose to go back toward safety or forward toward growth. Growth must be chosen again and again; fear must be overcome again and again."
-Abraham Maslow

~ ~ ~ ~

Write down any thoughts you may have regarding the poem or the quote.

_____

_____

_____

_____

_____

_____

_____

_____

_____

_____

How have you handled rejection in your life? How has it impacted you?

_____

_____

_____

_____

_____

_____

_____

_____

_____

_____

Teach Others

We're the best of the best,
So why mess with the rest?
If you want to succeed,
Put yourself through our test.

Want to travel through life,
With adventure and fame?
Jump on our wagon,
You'll never be the same.

Excitement and passion,
Is the life that we live.
And all that we do,
Is teach others to give.

"Learn from yesterday, live for today, hope for tomorrow."
-Albert Einstein

~ ~ ~ ~

Write down any thoughts you may have regarding the poem or the quote.

_____

_____

_____

_____

_____

_____

_____

_____

_____

_____

_____

What great life lesson have you learned and would share with someone? Why?

_____

_____

_____

_____

_____

_____

_____

_____

_____

_____

Health and Wellness

I am a balanced health and wellness coach,
We've developed a solid and unique approach.
I do my exercise with elastic bands,
Using only my legs and just my hands.

I can do it in my house,
Find health information with my mouse.
It can be done in the park,
Or by myself in the dark.

It's very simple, fast and easy,
My weight loss will happen quickly and breezy,
I'm getting healthy, fit and trim,
And in the near future I will be thin.

"The world can change in an instant. So can the way you choose to see it. Why not choose to see the good in yourself and others."

-Bob Perks

~ ~ ~ ~

Write down any thoughts you may have regarding the poem or the quote.

_____

_____

_____

_____

_____

_____

_____

_____

_____

_____

What are the things that you do well? How can your talents serve others?

_____

_____

_____

_____

_____

_____

_____

_____

_____

_____

_____

I Wish

I wish, I want
I need, I got!
This is how,
I direct my thoughts.

Loving the life,
That I now possess.
Taking the action required,
When I want to rest.

I wish, I want,
I need, I got!
A lesson learned,
And then to be taught.

"Without faith, we are lost, adrift in the world without an anchor."
-Rich DeVos

~ ~ ~ ~

Write down any thoughts you may have regarding the poem or the quote.

_____

_____

_____

_____

_____

_____

_____

_____

_____

_____

_____

What life lessons have you learned that would benefit others?

_____

_____

_____

_____

_____

_____

_____

_____

_____

_____

I Will Succeed

I'm happy, I'm healthy and financially free.
Those are the goals that I've set for me.

Decades of living, what a wonderful chance,
To dream of the future, and create a new dance.

It's the time to design, the rest of my life.
I chose winning, not just survival and strife.

The option of failure, does not exist.
I'm happy and healthy, because I persist.

I know what I want, I know that I can.
I'm consistent, persistent, and I've written my plan.

The success that I seek, I speak everyday.
My attitude's positive, and daily I pray.

I'm happy, I'm fit, and financially free.
This is the life that I envision for me.

I know it is possible, because I believe.
My life's an adventure, I know I'll succeed.

"A man can get discouraged many times, but he is not a failure until he begins to blame somebody else and stops trying."

-John Burroughs

~ ~ ~ ~

Write down any thoughts you may have regarding the poem or the quote.

_____

_____

_____

_____

_____

_____

_____

_____

_____

_____

_____

What are your goals spiritually, family, financial, physical, intellectual, emotional?

_____

_____

_____

_____

_____

_____

_____

_____

_____

_____

My Life

Life is a gift,
And meant to be lived.
So take your eyes off yourself,
And to others just give.

Life is my art,
To sculpt and to mold.
The canvas for life,
Is the dream that I hold.

Challenge and change,
I say, "Bring it on! Let's go!"
The bigger the challenge,
The greater I grow.

I face life's challenge
With excitement and thrill.
I see opportunity in change,
And my dreams I fulfill.

My life is my art,
And I'm in control.
Of all of the colors and images,
Until the final bell tolls.

"It is the heart always that sees, before the head can see."

-Thomas Carlyle

~ ~ ~ ~

Write down any thoughts you may have regarding the poem or the quote.

_____

_____

_____

_____

_____

_____

_____

_____

_____

_____

If your life is your art, how do you want to create it? What will you use?

_____

_____

_____

_____

_____

_____

_____

_____

_____

_____

_____

The Missing Sound

There's a sound that is missing,
Throughout the land today.
A sound that is gone,
I'm sorry to say.

There's a sound that is missing,
On our neighborhood streets.
No sound is more lovely,
Heartwarming or so sweet.

There is a sound that is missing,
And it's scary to think,
That of this beautiful sound,
Never again will we drink.

Where did it go?
It was here when I was a kid.
How could it leave,
When the children never did?

The sound that is missing,
Is the laughter and the shrieks,
Of all of our children,
Having fun playing in the streets.

The neighborhood's been taken over,
By adults who became scared and old.
Failing to teach the young
How to live a life that's bold.

So let's bring back the laughter,
the fun, the joy and song.
Let's get the kids into nature,
It's where they all belong.

"I am grateful for all of my problems. After each one was overcome, I became stronger and more able to meet those that were still to come. I grew in all my difficulties."

-J.C. Penney

~ ~ ~ ~

Write down any thoughts you may have regarding the poem or the quote.

_____

_____

_____

_____

_____

_____

_____

_____

_____

_____

_____

_____

What sounds seem to be missing in your life that you would like to recapture?

_____

_____

_____

_____

_____

_____

_____

_____

_____

_____

_____

What a Zoo

I'm fighting the traffic,
My God, what a zoo!
Millions of people,
Wondering what else they could do.

Millions of people,
To the job they do drive.
Some seeking freedom,
Most only to survive.

Sitting in traffic,
Going from home to the job.
Knowing to well,
That they're just being robbed.

For years they will perform,
This social behavior.
Never seeking to change,
Or shift the tide in their favor.

"I couldn't wait for success, so I went ahead without it."
-Jonathan Winters

~ ~ ~ ~

Write down any thoughts you may have regarding the poem or the quote.

_____

_____

_____

_____

_____

_____

_____

_____

_____

_____

What have you been waiting for that you know you should move forward with?

_____

_____

_____

_____

_____

_____

_____

_____

_____

_____

A Generation

Once there was a generation, that believed they had it all.
Fast cars and houses, and shopping at malls.
Once they were hippies, then boomers they became.
Living a life that for years before, they had disdained.

They fought for their causes, created a cultural revolution.
Raised human rights issues and fought for solutions.
Then one day they awoke, and much to their surprise,
They realized too late, they were victims of their own demise.

You see, what had happened, was they were deeply in debt,
To the system they had fought, but it fact did forget.
They put away the flowers and headbands they wore,
And stopped fighting for causes, it had become such a chore.

They retired to the couches and their Lazy Boy chairs,
Now evenings and weekends, at the TV they stare.
They're disgruntled with their future, and forgot what they had,
So day after day they repeat, and it's really quite sad.

Yet, I do believe, there are some who have found,
They can change the world, and create something profound.
They know it's not easy, something worthwhile never will be,
Through persistence and passion the dream they will see.

"No matter how bad someone has it, there are others who have it worse. Remembering that makes life a lot easier and allows you to take pleasure in the blessings you have been given."

-Lou Holtz

~ ~ ~ ~

Write down any thoughts you may have regarding the poem or the quote.

_____

_____

_____

_____

_____

_____

_____

_____

_____

_____

_____

What blessings have you been given that you should be grateful for, but have forgotten?

_____

_____

_____

_____

_____

_____

_____

_____

_____

_____

A Ritual Not to Miss

At the end of the day we say goodnight,
Give a hug, a squeeze and a kiss.
All these years we've come to learn,
This ritual not to miss.

Every morning as I leave,
A hug, a squeeze another kiss.
All these years we've come to learn,
This ritual not to miss.

"Happiness is like a kiss. You must share it to enjoy it"
-Bernard Meltzer

~ ~ ~ ~

Write down any thoughts you may have regarding the poem or the quote.

_____

_____

_____

_____

_____

_____

_____

_____

_____

_____

What ritual could you start today that would make your relationships better?

_____

_____

_____

_____

_____

_____

_____

_____

_____

_____

Just a Few Thoughts

I travelled along with a flying dragon,
Blue and black its wings a waggin'.
Ziggin' here and zaggin' there,
On the winds of life without a care.

I've traveled along with a pel-i-can,
If a bird can fly surely I can!
On a bike or boat or motor car,
Traveling with creatures I feel so on par.

Swimming deep beneath the sea,
All God's creatures inspire me.
I've dived Aruba and Bonaire,
As well as Curacao, without a care.

The Cayman Islands shared their treasures,
And with each dive life enhanced my pleasures.
I traveled deep into a mountain glen,
I've seen the great bald eagle and singing wren.

I've hiked the Grand Canyon with tears of joy,
While my wife was pregnant with my little boy.
I've traveled throughout most of the U.S. of A,
With more lands to see and songs to play.

Yes, I've been blessed I must admit,
To a life of adventure I still commit.
Life is grand and short as well,
These are just a few thoughts I had to tell.

"It is not in the stars to hold our destiny but in ourselves"
-William Shakespeare

~ ~ ~ ~

Write down any thoughts you may have regarding the poem or the quote.

_____

_____

_____

_____

_____

_____

_____

_____

_____

_____

What adventure have you been putting off that would be meaningful and fulfilling to you?

_____

_____

_____

_____

_____

_____

_____

_____

_____

_____

Friends

One thing I have come to realize,
As I journey on my quest.
True friends are rare,
But are found when you least expect.

Final Thoughts

Take a few moments and write down any stray thoughts, ideas or transform-ations you thought you would get to later. I hope that you have enjoyed this little bit of my life and that something that I have written has inspired you to take action in a new direction in your life. Life is an amazing adventure that encompasses challenges, peaks and valleys. I hope that as you travel on your journey that you will find love, joy, health and happiness.

www.ingramcontent.com/pod-product-compliance
Lightning Source LLC
Chambersburg PA
CBHW081230090426
42738CB00016B/3247